There was no path So I trod one.

Poems by
Edwina Gateley

SOURCE BOOKS
TRABUCO CANYON
CALIFORNIA

© Edwina Gateley 1996
Cover picture by Chris Shepherd
Photographs © Jane Clarke
Typesetting & Design, Studio 185

First Printing 1996
Reprinted, 2000

Library of Congress CIP Data

Gateley, Edwina.
There was no path, so I trod one : poems / by Edwina Gateley.
p. cm.
Includes index.
ISBN 0-940147-40-8 (trade paper)
1. Christian poetry, American.   I. Title.
PS3557 . A859T48   1996
811' .54--dc20   96–3658
                                                        CIP

ISBN 0–940147–40–8

Published by:

SOURCE BOOKS
Box 794
Trabuco Canyon   CA 92678

Printed by KNI Inc., Anaheim   CA

Dedication

To Julie and Elise
whose creation of 'Morningstar',
a retreat space for women
in the woods and wild spaces of Michigan,
provides for me and many
a place of beauty and solitude
to write and dream and play.

Contents

Introduction

My first book of religious and spiritual poetry *Psalms of A Laywoman* was published in 1981, and none of us imagined that fifteen years later it would be in its seventh printing and continue to be in demand. The hunger for 'soul poetry' is timeless and insatiable. Religious and spiritual poetry speaks to the human soul which links us all and touches that seed of divine longing which remains hidden in our busy and anxious lives. In all of us there is a longing—however deeply hidden—for solitude, mystery and awe. It is as if a mystic lies slumbering in each of us who, from time to time, is stirred and aroused through experiences of pain, passion, grief or any deeply felt emotion. It is a depth of which, for the most part, we are not a little afraid: for where the mystic slumbers there is repressed passion and intensity of emotion which surely disturbs our everyday lives.

When we are open to this depth we touch the God who dwells at the core of our vulnerability. It is like falling into the center of meaning: everything else is eclipsed as we are swept onto a soul plane where, for a moment or two, we are suffused in mystery and awe. Passion carries us. Physically we no longer exist. We enter into deep insights and the soul cries out.

Such an experience must, of its nature, pass quickly as we taste the divine at the heart of human existence. This experience is not uncommon, but its articulation is. The mystical event is expressed in religious or spiritual poetry—one of the few special mediums whereby such experiences can be shared adequately.

Spiritual and religious poetry leaves the poet vulnerable, because the visions of the soul and the traumas of the heart are laid bare for all to read. At the same time they belong to all of us, and must be shared so we might draw a little closer to one another on our inevitably lonely journeys towards deeper human understanding and oneness.

I have selected these poems as the most direct expressions of experiencing the divine during my work. Many are from my previously published books: thirty are from *I Hear A Seed Growing,* eleven from *Psalms of a Laywoman,* and five from *A Warm Moist Salty God.* Of these, several poems have been reprinted elsewhere in liturgical pamphlets, community newsletters, and so on. The balance of the poems is new, arising from my life and ministry during the last two years.

The arrangement here of the poems under sub-headings is fairly arbitrary, but it may be helpful to those who are looking for a thematic reading for liturgical use or personal reflection.

I pray that this collection of poetry will speak to your heart and stir within you a recognition of the slumbering mystic which dwells at the core of your being. May we continue to listen to the cries of the heart which guide us on our journey as we stumble together towards the divine.

Edwina Gateley
Michigan, 1996

Quiet Spaces

Adirondack

There is a chair
a heavy grey Adirondack
that sits alone
and empty
upon a hilltop
surrounded by
wild brush and
sprouting things.
In all weathers it stands
firmly rooted
to the lonely patch
of woodland
as if it had been thrust up
from the earth
like a tree.
Little creatures sit
upon its broad arms,
nibbling and scratching,
insects weave and scuttle
in its joints.
And I am awed
before its silent invitation.
its fierce beckoning
to slip into its woody embrace
and stay,
held there,
in its solidity.
Sacred it sits
in its leafy solitude
and I, secular,
slip away quietly:
Unwilling to surrender.

We must make spaces

We must make spaces
in our lives
for quiet gentle times,
to remind us that
all is gift,
and blessing flows
through our lives
as we expect and
recognize it
woven in
our heart beats

Morningstar

Wondrous place.
Set aside
like a chosen delicacy
to be savored and tasted
in dusky solitude.
A place where few venture,
for paths are not well trod,
and the earth is rough and harsh.
Only little wild creatures,
scrabbling for food in the undergrowth,
disturb the awesome silence.
But, of a sudden, one will find
amongst the red and rock–strewn land,
delicate lumps of lime green moss
stretched out like shaggy rugs
thick and springing beneath one's feet.
And,
through the clusters of tall gray trees,
the sun, all golden and diffuse,
like God,
casts pure light
on dark emptiness.

Silent God

Silent God,
empty, sound-less,
like the long, dark nights
without life,
I wait, gently hoping,
for your touch which says,
"I'm here."
But the void remains,
Unfilled.
Silent God,
Why do you hide your face
from me?
Why withhold your breath
which kindles life?
Why, God, silent God,
do you watch your loved one,
alone and waiting
yet not reach out,
to only whisper:
"I am here"?
Yet I will wait
and I will watch,
and in my mind's eye,
soaring deep from my soul,
I will see and
I will know—
You are here.

The Retreat

I came from
the clamoring voices,
the noise, the speed,
the action.
I came from
the city's heat
the crowds, the traffic
the fraction.

I came to
the deep deep snow
and the watching trees
so still.
I came to
the vast domed sky,
the lonely
empty hill.

I came to a moist
and generous place
to feed my soul awhile.
To be hugged
by God's great bosom
and sleep,
deep,
beneath her smile.

The Seed

The seed grows and bears fruit
not because of our talents and gifts
but because we leave space in
our darkness for God to take root

Morning Prayers

Just A Little Difference

Ah—a resting place,
where we come to understand
it is not required of us
to wrestle constantly and passionately
with our God—
nor pursue relentlessly
all God's decrees as we understand them,
but only that we listen and wonder
and hope and pray,
that we might, perhaps,
make just a little difference,
one quiet grey day.

Changes

Dear God
Be with me,
as I walk your paths
In places I sometimes
do not want to go.
Be with me
as I say goodbye
to those I want
to stay with.
Be with me
as I leave behind gifts
so newly given and
hardly seen.
Be with me
as I try,
sometimes sadly,
to walk
your way.

Let Me

Let me walk with you
even if I must walk alone,
and in the dark.

Let me hear your whisper
even when my noise and clatter resounds
through day and dusk.

Let me be praying
even when my whole being flees restless
from your presence.

Let me be faithful
even when, afraid and helpless,
I want to go my way.

Oh God! Please,
just let me learn
to be with you.

God Dance

Living God,
let me flow
with the waters,
fly with the wind
and shine
with the stars.
Let me round
with the moon
and stretch
with the sky.
And in my dance,
Living God,
let me become
the waters, the moon,
the wind and the stars
dancing and leaping
through the universe
Clear and shining
dancing your name.

Pull Me Through

Pull me through, dear God—
just pull me through
once more,
because I'm stuck and
it's dark, dear God—
just give me
a little pull,
Because there is no space
down here
and I cannot see
the sky.
Just give me
a little pull, dear God—
only a little pull,
for I want to smell the morning rain
and feel the cold,
free breeze.
Oh, give me a little pull,
dear God,
just a little pull.

Feminine Wisdom

She rose from the shadows,
ancient, magnificent,
cloaked in soft brown wool
that smelt of moist earth,
her eyes shone deep wet
reflecting the wisdom
of ages past, and present,
and yet to come.
She held a rounded stone
which shone like crystal
and a yellow-black serpent
hugged her sapped bosom.
Ah, she rose from the shadows
of ancient history
into the consciousness
of millions of souls seeking
wholeness, harmony and hope,
longing for the wisdom
of the great sleeping mother.
She rose from the shadows,
ancient, magnificent
and the belly of the ocean
stirred
as humanity
groaned in her birthing.

Let Your God Love You

Be silent,
Be still.
Alone.
Empty
Before your God.
Say nothing.
Ask nothing.
Be silent.
Be still.
Let your God
Look upon you.
That is all.
God knows
And understands.
God loves you with
An enormous love.
Wanting only to
Look upon you
With Love.
Quiet
Still.
Be.

Let your God—
Love you.

Abba

Abba, Father
I love You!
Abba, Mother,
I thank You.
Abba, Father,
I am not afraid.
So let me walk
Your way
Wherever it may lead.
Only Holy One—
Go before me.

Last Song

I sat,
caressed by the coolness
of the Spring sun
and listened to a solitary sound
that carried the night.

Loud and sharp
against the silence
rang the glorious notes
of a late, lone bird,
full throttled as she sang
her last splendid song,
leaving my small mind
entranced and awe-struck
as darkness fell and
stilled the listening forest.

God Whispers

Small Deeps

We are too complicated.
We seek God here, there and everywhere.
We seek God in holy places, in books,
in rules, regulations, rites and rituals.
We seek God in pomp and glory and
ceremony,
in relics and statues
and visions and shrines.
We seek God in Popes and Fathers
and saints.
Ah, like lost bewildered children,
we seek the God
who waits to be found
in the small deeps
of the human heart.

Be Glad

God is soaked
in our world.
God's Spirit
lives and breathes
in and through
all that is.
We are lost
only when we
do not understand
that God
is already with
and in
each one of us.
Our task is recognition
of God's initiative
to be at home in us—
acceptance
of God–With–Us.
Then we cannot but
be glad.

It Seems To Me

It seems to me
that God
chooses to snuggle
deep in our souls;
Stirring from time to time,
to nudge
our dimmed awareness
of divinity
enmeshed
in our guts.

Glimpsing God

I catch a glimpse,
Now and then,
Of God.
A swift passing
Sweetness
Which makes light the hour,
the day, the week.
Elusive, inconstant,
Yet never totally absent
From the hurtling days with
Their shadows.
I grieve
That such a beautiful
Awareness,
Like an unexpected visitor,
Comes infrequently,
Entertains briefly,
And passes
With a whisper.
Is lost then
In the laughter
And the music
Of the night.

A Warm, Moist, Salty God

Deep in the forest
I found my God
leaping through the trees,
spinning with the glancing sunlight,
caressing with the breeze.
There where the grasses
rose and fell
fanning the perfumed air,
I smelt her beauty,
elusive, free,
dancing everywhere.

Deep in the city
I found my God
weeping in the bar,
prowling beneath the glaring lights,
dodging speeding car.
There where the women
were pimped and raped,
cursing for a light,
I felt her presence,
fierce, deep,
sobbing in the night.

Deep in myself
I found my God
stirring in my guts,
quickening my middle-aged bones,
stilling all my buts.
There where my spirit
had slumbered long,
numbed into a trance,
A moist, warm, salty God
arose,
and beckoned me to Dance.

Gentle God

God is breathing gently,
God never hurries,
Is never anxious or pressing,
God just waits,
Breathing gently upon us
With great tenderness
Until we look to God—
And, knowingly,
Nod.

God Ran Away

God ran away
when we imprisoned her
and put her in a box
named Church
God would have none
of our labels and
our limitations
and said,
"I will escape and plant myself
in a simpler, poorer soil
where those who see, will see,
and those who hear, will hear.
I will become a God—believable,
because I am free,
and go where I will.
My goodness will be found
in the freedom I offer to all—
regardless of color, sex or status,
regardless of power or money.
Ah, I am God
because I am free
and all those who would be free
will find me,
roaming, wandering, singing.
Come, walk with me—
come, dance with me!
I created you to sing—to dance—
to love..."

If you cannot sing,
nor dance, nor love,
because they put you
also in a box,
know that your God broke free
and ran away.
So, send your spirit
then, to dance
with the God
whom they cannot tame nor chain.
Dance within, though they chain
your very guts
to the great stone walls...
Dance, beloved,
Ah, Dance!

Made Holy

We are made holy
by our recognition
of God in us.

God is in all and everything.
But the reality of
God's presence
only comes about
through human recognition.
Ah then!
We have the power
to sacralize the world.

Silent God

This is my prayer—
That, though I may not see,
I be aware
Of the Silent God
Who stands by me.
That, though I may not feel,
I be aware
Of the Mighty Love
Which doggedly follows me.
That, though I may not respond,
I be aware
That God—my Silent, Mighty God,
Waits each day.
Quietly, hopefully, persistently,
Waits each day and through each night
For me,
For me—alone.

Tell Them

Breaking through the powers of darkness
bursting from the stifling tomb
he slipped into the graveyard garden
to smell the blossomed air.

Tell them, Mary, Jesus said,
that I have journeyed far
into the darkest deeps I've been
in nights without a star.

Tell them, Mary, Jesus said,
that fear will flee my light
that though the ground will tremble
and despair will stalk the earth
I hold them firmly by the hand
through terror to new birth.

Tell them, Mary, Jesus said,
the globe and all that's made
is clasped to God's great bosom
they must not be afraid
for though they fall and die, he said,
and the black earth wrap them tight
they will know the warmth
of God's healing hands
in the early morning light.

Tell them, Mary, Jesus said,
smelling the blossomed air,
tell my people to rise with me
and heal the Earth's despair.

God In The Brothel

I went to the brothel
and took God
with me.
The Madam cursed and spat
fury and hatred,
spewing it out
all over the kitchen
and all over God.
The ladies sat listless,
in dreadful despair,
waiting for the customers,
with their dirty minds,
and cold, cold lust.
The men,
furtive and awkward,
in their smart business suits,
itching to rape,
and to steal,
before driving home
to the wife and kids,
and barbecue
on the lawn.
I went to the brothel
and found God
within.
And, through all
the sickness,
the sin, and
the stink,
God sat,
in stunned and dreadful
silence.

Enough

What do you say?
What can you say?
Why, nothing,
For this is another world
Whose ways are different,
Whose faces are
Awesome,
Full of mystery, and awful knowledge,
And unknown fears.
What is their language?
I cannot speak of
Books and poetry,
Food or fashions.
I cannot debate about
God or morality,
Ministry or celebration.
I can only sit
Dumb and helpless—
A child,
Untutored to a world of
Street and brothel
And shelter.
Their faces are fixed
And silent,
Carved into lines of
Pain
By years of wind and
Snow and dirty sidewalks.
They shuffle, slouch and
Drag themselves from
Shelter to shelter,
And stand in
Weary derelict lines

Outside the soup kitchen,
Where cheery well-fed
Youngsters
Excitedly prepare the
Rice and cabbage for
The hungry poor.
An experience.
To feed the hungry—
Just like Jesus said.
They take turns,
Come in bus loads,
Each week
A different group.
But the faces in
The lines are always
The same.
No 'experience' for them.
They are not interested in
The hand that
Feeds them,
Only want
To fix that aching belly
With swimming cabbage.
They are silent,
Only the coughs and
Spitting to he heard.
They have learnt
To he silent
Before the stark horror
And bleakness of
Their lives.
Dirty sidewalks,
Swimming cabbage,

continued

The dreary basement shelter.
Ah, great and gentle God!
Will you be silent too?
Or will your Kingdom
Erupt,
Scattering cabbage and garbage
All over the basement floor?
Will you reach out,
Oh, great and gentle God,
Letting your tears
Cleanse and heal
The dirty bodies,
The broken hearts?
Oh, great and gentle God
Will you cry aloud and
Crush the rat and the cockroach?
Will you sob,
'Enough!'
Will you?
Will you?
Great and gentle God.

The Birthing

They said I could not celebrate
For woman I was born.
They said I couldn't proclaim or preach
For woman I was born.
They said no worship I could lead
For woman I was born.
Then they closed the door and said no more
For woman I was born.

So woman born, I crept away,
Into a silent place
And stretched my woman body
On the naked moist cold earth.
There, cradled by the darkness,
Beneath a purple sky
I opened wide my woman legs
And heaved an anguished cry.
Then from my woman body slipped
The tiny perfect form
Of the One they call the Living God—
Of woman body born.

The Not Yet Born

Volcano—Volcano.
Bubbling rich red.
Steaming.
Spirit—creation
Bursting. Bursting
For release and life.

And I must
Carry you
Hot and aching
Within me
Until your time
Is come.

Mysterious,
Lonely gestation,
Formed in darkness.
Fed and nurtured
By a life and spirit
Breathing gently, powerfully
In my soul.
Hush. Silence.
The time is
Not yet.
Now is only
Slow murmurings and
Gentle stirrings.
Oh! Not yet born!
But how you live!

I love you, Volcano.
I love your
Sweeping pain and
Thrusting, tentative movement.

I love you, Volcano,
As you sleep and wait
Within me
For your life.
And for your death.

Mother God

Mother
I love you.
My belly aches
for you—
sweet agony!
I cannot fill this hunger,
slake this thirst.
It broods
untouched,
utterly real,
within me.
I cannot calm
nor comfort
this deep
and ancient longing
to sink home into
your vast embrace
your hot, hot
belly.
Mother
I love you.

Prayers & Screams

The Picnic

They sat on the church's stone steps
right on the corner where four roads meet
while anxious traffic sped and hooted past,
five middle-aged women dressed in assorted
mismatched clothes and oversized shoes.
Parked on the sidewalk, within easy reach,
stood their supermarket carts,
piled high with paper, bottles,
and beloved garbage.

The women, oblivious to the roar of traffic,
did not care it was now the early hours
of the morning,
and everyone was rushing home
to bed and shelter.

With loving, fastidious care,
they placed a tall plastic bottle of ginger ale
on the center step—
and around it, five plastic cartons,
collected in the day
and washed in McDonald's restrooms.
Then, with self-satisfaction and decorum,
they poured out the ale into the cartons.
"Half full for everybody," one said.
The ale was passed around.
The ladies grasped it
and supped the special treat—
trophy of the day's hunting.

Then followed a dozen compliments
on the quality and sparkle
of the night's ale.

A few jokes, light-hearted comments—
The darkness grew thicker, the traffic lulled,
and, cradling the plastic cartons,
sensing the growing cold,
and the utter loneliness
of the empty bottle,
a terrible sadness took possession of
the five middle-aged ladies,
partners of the night,
and from their heaving souls broke out
a mighty silent scream.

God is big.

Silent Presence

I thought that God
Had come to me.
That after the wild delights
And the suffering and the joys
And the pain and the hopelessness
Of the years—
That God
Had come to me.
That after adventure and achievement,
Pain, despair and death,
God
Had come to me.
Yes—with relief and mild surprise
I met my God again.
And then I saw,
Oh, fool, I saw!
That God had suffered
The pain and hopelessness,
Had shared the achievements and the joys,
That God,
All enveloping,
All compassion,
Had there been silence
All the time.

Today

I have seen
no joy
today
and seen
no hope
today,
but experienced
a little faith.

Healing

The pain and the wounds
go too deep
for us to heal
alone.
Only God,
only a
far Greater Power
can penetrate
such depth
of pain,
and gently, gently,
sooth,
and kiss us into
wholeness.
It is too much
for us,
all of it has to be
given over
entirely
to God.
All of it.

Only an empty soul can be filled.

Dreaming

Why do I keep on searching?
Dogged, dogged.
Always longing for something more,
believing in a new potential,
grasping the fragment of a dream,
a vision
barely glimpsed.
Why am I so pursued
by Spirit thrusting in my belly,
rising whilst I sleep
and stirring stilled waters.
So I wander
like one lost and mad
across thirsty deserts and
silent forests,
tracing lonely paths
in solitary places
being hurled back
into the city streets,
carrying within me
a groaning
Woman God,
longing and terrified
to be born.

The Creative Potential of the Dead End

I have come up against
a wall—
a blank—
nowhere to go—
unsure, lost—
bewildered.
Creativity is released
in any death,
when we believe in life,
when we are people of hope.
For people of hope
there is never any real death
for death has been conquered by Christ
and life has been exchanged for it.
I have faced death often
in many different ways
and everything has seemed hopeless
life–less.
At the moment of death I am called
to a faith response
that defies reason.
If only we had even a scrap
of resurrection faith,
there would be an abundance
of life and hope.

We turn away too often
in despair
in hopelessness
in tiredness
in anger
in self–pity
in defeat.
We turn away from the Dead–End
the tomb,
because we are blind.
We fail to see the light
waiting to be called forth
in resurrection.
Jesus saw his dead–end coming.
Everything he worked and preached for
was crumbling around him.
The whole thing
was in a shambles;
his followers scared and confused,
but he never turned back,
even when he got to the dead–end
—he walked right into it in faith,
and he destroyed death
and dead-ends.

Going Home

Letting go again...
The time is fast coming
And, I know,
I will never
be prepared for
the wrenching farewells
the spaces left and
the sad betrayed faces.
No.
It will not be easy
to leave the world and space
I have wandered in so long,
wrestled with,
hated and loved
so passionately.
Yet, deep in my guts
I know
this place is not
my own,
and I, no longer,
am a wanderer.
It is almost time
to take
the last journey
home.

There is life,
there is nourishment
down there
in that darkness.

We Tell Our
Stories

In Memory of Maria

Earth sister and
late Autumnal mother
you were to me, dear friend.
Touching and quickening
my slumbering heart cells
with your gentle wisdom.
Ah—I remember
your great green eyes,
pools of vitality
that flashed and leapt
with love and joy
so many, many times
leaving others (small timid hearts),
amazed and embarrassed
at your expansiveness.
Deep listener,
you took into yourself
the trembling anguish
of battered souls,
holding them gently
in your arms,
soaking up their tears
into your mother self.
Dancing woman
Leaping and sparkling!
Your heavy and splendid body
caught in the drumming
of the Latin beat.
Ah! You left us all behind
in the trail of your
southern magic.
And when you were invited
to a reception
for the Pope

in the patriarchal palace,
you dared to wear
a shining dress of red
and a flower in your hair.
You claimed and bore your
rich feminine self amongst
the black–robed priests
who clutched their celibacy
in terror before your bursting womanhood.
Ah! Autumnal mother,
your song has penetrated
thick grey walls and
shattered prison doors where the poor and
little ones crept out, weeping,
to hear your music.
But in the grey closing
of a winter night
you died too soon,
my sister,
your dazzling eyes—veiled,
dancing body—stilled
and your oh,
so listening ears
fell deaf to
the sobs around you.
Ah, dear friend,
Autumnal mother,
how I grieve
the lost magic
of your presence,
and stilling of your song
and your gentle, oh so gentle,
slipping away
from me.

To Maria

So now, dear friend,
have you slipped from my warm embrace
into the gentle arms of death.
So quietly, almost gratefully,
letting go the years of long journeying
that drew tears and song from the deeps
of your woman soul.
Ah, dear friend,
so softly you surrendered
the dazzling dreams
that led you dancing and weeping round
the universe.

And now, dear friend,
your warm woman body that,
rich and radiant, drew all eyes,
is but a scattering of ashes
that whisper through my fingers
falling soft as snow onto
the earth and crumbling leaves.
Ah, now dear friend,
your bones that so embraced the world
and loved to tread its many paths,
(dancing all the while)
lie held in the moist damp earth
nuzzled by the first thrustings
of early summer seeds.

Ah, now dear friend,
have you become
the earth you loved and danced upon.
Ah, woman–body, ever giving,
now like a soothing carpet
are you laid beneath our weary feet
whilst your spirit, dear friend,
urges on the new young blooms
leaping still with joy
at the great Spring Birthing.

The Stars That Shone Wet

You were taken—
snatched away in the night,
and I was left
trembling, bereft,
to continue the journey
without your song.
On this new lonely road
the clamor of many voices
assail me.
They knock at my
bruised heart and
pull at my skirts
acclaiming and proclaiming,
close possessing.
But a tiny stillness
sits steadfast
curled in my belly,
never to be stirred
nor touched by
intruding forces—
the deep joyous memory
of the stars
that shone wet
in your eyes.
Ah—blessed gift!
I clutch within my soul
the stars
that shone wet
in your eyes.

I will always love
you.

Love Song

I'll see you again in
the breaking of the Spring,
I'll walk with you again
when the song birds sing
I'll laugh with you again
when the creek runs free
and together we will dance
around the budded tree.

I'll hold you in my heart, dear friend,
till the bitter winds are gone
I'll cradle your soft fragile dreams
and sing a gentle song,
and we will live again, my friend,
to dance o'er stars and moon
and roll amongst the daisies
when the Spring breaks in new bloom.

Dolores

Dolores,
dear one.
With your chewed-up,
over-kissed
teddy bear
stuffed in your pocket.
Dolores,
dear one,
with your new young dreams,
trailing in bits
behind you.
Dolores,
dear one,
lumbering up the Broadway,
drowning your
knots of despair,
in deep,
red wine.
Dolores,
dear one—
don't die.

The Sharing

We told our stories—
That's all.
We sat and listened to
Each other
And heard the journeys
Of each soul.
We sat in silence
Entering each one's pain and
Sharing each one's joy.
We heard love's longing
And the lonely reachings—out
For love and affirmation.
We heard of dreams
Shattered
And visions fled.
Of hopes and laughter
Turned stale and dark.
We felt the pain of
Isolation and
The bitterness
Of death.

But in each brave and
Lonely story
God's gentle life
Broke through
And we heard music in
The darkness
And smelt flowers in
The void.

We felt the budding
Of creation
In the searchings of
Each soul
And discerned the beauty
Of God's hand in
Each muddy, twisted path.

And God's voice sang
In each story
God's life sprang from
Each death.
Our sharing became
One story
Of a simple lonely search
For life and hope and
Oneness
In a world which sobs
For love.
And we knew that in our sharing
God's voice with
Mighty breath
Was saying
Love each other and
Take each other's hand.

For you are one
Though many
And in each of you
I live.
So listen to my story
And share my pain
And death.
Oh, listen to my story
And rise and live
With me.

Joe White Eagle

Joe White Eagle
staggered into the basement shelter
drunk and stinking.
A red woolen hat
was pulled over
his half–closed blackened eye,
and his dirty sweater was
frayed and too short.
He wore baggy trousers
that shone
with years of grease.
Staggering,
grinning,
eyes unfocused,
Joe White Eagle
marked a cross
on the Sign–in Sheet,
and dragged
his thin foam mattress
towards the center of
the basement floor.
The coffee in the
fragile styrofoam cup
spilled onto the cement floor,
as Joe
bent clumsily forward
to pull off his heavy
lace–less boots.
"Ah—what the hell,"

He gave up and
collapsed, exhausted,
fully clothed, on
the mattress and
the styrofoam cup
All around him
the foul smell of
unwashed bodies
and dirty clothes
arose, and filled
the basement shelter.
Coughing, spluttering,
spitting, snoring...
The homeless and
the derelicts
fell into
troubled, lonely sleep.
Joe White Eagle,
derelict,
bum,
drunk,
sprawled in a pitiful heap
on the shelter's
cold grey floor,
senseless,
pathetic figure
of utter despair, and
degradation.
Morning came.

continued

It was a sharp,
cold day.
Only the gulls
and a lone jogger
broke the still air
with movement.
The lake was hushed and flat,
filled with millions
of sparkling suns.
The breeze
barely whispered
over the vast
shining waters.
Etched darkly
against the silver lake,
great and bottomless,
in a lotus position,
a lonely figure sat,
lost
inside himself,
absorbed in
another world,
another life,
swept up in
the deep of the lake and
the vastness of the sky.
A sudden breeze
playfully brushed
his dark shining hair

and there,
bronzed and noble,
face lifted up
to the pale, pale sun,
Joe White Eagle
sat
proud and un–surrendered,
son and brother,
of his native land and lake.
Joe White Eagle,
hunter and warrior
of the great empty plains,
lost in a thousand dreams
of dignity and
dying splendor.
Joe White Eagle sat
proud and un–surrendered.

Child Sleeping

I watched him sleeping,
his skin, still baby soft
as velvet, brushing
my roughened fingers.
I imagined
the coarsening
the hardening
the bristling
that would come
with the seasons.
And I knew with a pang
that I would miss
the softness of my baby's skin
its feathery whispering
against my goodnight kiss.
I marvelled at
the rich dark glow
of my baby's cheek,
at the beauty of his
earth browness.
And a chill crept round my soul,
an instinctive fierce longing
to protect forever
my precious bronzed child
against small-minded people
drained white and bloodless
through fear and hatred.
I watched my baby sleeping
soft and brown and fresh from God
And I knew
as I stroked his tight black curls,
the passion and the terror
of a jealous primordial love.

Addict Beloved

I saw in her glassed stare
the fierce resistance
of the addict, bent on
engaging the world in
blood–less battle
to stake indisputable claim
to the cancerous chemical
that fed on her wasted body.
Like death partners,
they clung together
in jealous passion
and possession.

I saw in her glassed stare,
vacant and terrible,
a woman I once thought I knew,
who, vibrant and vital
had leapt into the world
with hot embrace
and myriad longings.

I saw in her glassed stare
the broken dreams
tattered vision and
lost laughter
of a generation of
frightened children.

I saw in her glassed stare,
wild and darkening,
my own reflection—
horror struck,
shattered,
staring back.

Oma

Oma was found dead in
her run-down hotel room.
She had been dead
three days.
I loved old Oma,
one-eyed street lady
from Alabama.
Wrinkled tired face like
a dried up prune,
Thin as a pole,
alcoholic, and
beautiful in her gentleness.

Oma—
One blue eye looking out,
terrified,
at an uncaring world,

Oma—
Laughing so readily
through all her pain,
chain smoking,
longing to be a lady
in the slums and the violence of
her inner-city world,
peopled with lonely
and bewildered homeless—
like herself.

Oma—
So proud to have found
a room of her own,
at last.
So proud of the dark, cracked walls
because they were hers
to die in.

Stanley

The police shot Stanley today—
in self-defence, they said.
I remember Stanley well—
A young effeminate man,
who wore floral shirts
and tight cut-off jeans.
He was a prostitute,
a gentle, hurting man,
looking for love,
down the back alleys.
Stanley's eyes would light up
when we met
at the busy intersection.
He would fling his arms around me
and tell me I was beautiful.
He would do a little dance of joy,
when I told him,
he, too, was beautiful.
Stanley never did fit into
his harsh and violent world.
His floral shirt and cheap bracelets
were incongruous
amidst the garbage and rage
of the streets where he wandered.
Stanley, elegant, beautiful,
and so, so alone
lying in a pool.
Three bullets through his smooth chest.

I think, had I been there
before the pistols fired,
Stanley would have clasped his arms
around me
sobbing, sobbing.
There would have been a flood of tears,
instead of a pool of blood

The Peroxide Hooker

Down the alley
The peroxide hooker
Dove furtively in search
Of a quick job
For five bucks
(Used to be ten—
But times are hard
And we can't be choosey).
The decoy cop cruised up
And beckoned to
The peroxide hooker,
To hassle for the price
And the service to be given...
She shot for ten and then
In desperation...five.
The badge was flashed
And spitting and snarling,
To bite back tears,
The peroxide hooker was
Bundled in the back seat
And sped triumphantly
To the big red jail
We built for her.
We put prison bars around her
And high tiled walls,
So we would not see
The peroxide hooker cry
And spit on us
In grief turned to fury
And pain turned to hate.

We nailed her to our public cross
And, shaking our heads,
Tutting her sin,
We left the hooker
To die alone
In the shame that
She was born in.
We turned away
From the peroxide hooker
And fled to the dark safety
Of the sacred church walls
To pray for God's mercy
For the woman on the cross.
To pray for God's mercy
For the woman on the cross.

Stella

I found her scrunched up—
Like a polyester ball,
On the church steps.
It was April and cold,
And well past midnight.
Her grey hair was dishevelled,
Like her face,
And her torn pop-socks
Had fallen in little bunches
Around her ankles.
She clutched her large plastic bag
Filled with garbage,
Made precious by possession.
"Where are we going?" She cried,
As she clutched my hand,
And her garbage,
Scuttling bowlegged, along
The dirty street.
Ah, Stella—
Tiny, deaf and toothless—
Away, away from the 'House of God,'
And the shame of your bed on its steps.
Away, away from this dark smelly street,
That's become your home and bedroom.
Away, away from the passers-by
Looking the other way,
In dark, embarrassed ignorance.
Ah, Stella, Stella
Tiny, deaf and toothless,
Away, away from a church unworthy
Of your precious, precious garbage...

Rape of Ages

Like the weight
of deep waters
I carry within me
a great soul pain.
My womb
sobbing and weeping
for my many
child sisters
raped and beaten
through the ages.
In the weight of
the deep waters
my woman–womb
trembles for
the girl babies born
onto hungry male violence.
Like thundering waves
their cries arise
from the earth,
calling aloud for
the Ancient Crone,
Woman Wisdom,
the Mother of all ages,
in whose warm waters
they first swam in
primordial peace and blessing.
Ah,
the waters that once circled with love
the soft girl bodies
now weigh, brooding,
around the closed unseeded womb,
deeply deeply
angry.

Earth

Snow

Lead like,
sullen yellow,
the wet sky pressed down
upon the rows of clapboard houses
and the grey pot-holed streets
where children and garbage
rolled and played
hiding and crouching
in the gutters.
In the dustiness of
the winter twilight
the breeze dropped
and a stillness
fell upon the clapboard houses
the grey pot-holed streets
and the rolling garbage.
Silent,
like death,
the sky fell
and claimed it all,
enveloping
humanity's drabness
in a hushed and
gentle shroud of white, white snow.
Cold, soft and unrelenting
it stole upon the city,
leaving the gathered
balls of garbage shimmering
in sparkling hillocks of
silver beauty.

The Massacre of Forests

The wind told the trees
of the massacre of their brothers,
deep down in the far south of the land.

The wind saw it, and screeched and cried,
driving herself northward
with the tale of destruction
howling in her billows.

And the trees of the north shook and
rocked in the embrace of the wind;
Heavens and roots trembled
at the senseless acts of human greed.

The wind gentled, whispered away,
leaving the trees standing stark,
stretched out, all–knowing,
grieving against the reddened sky.

Did anyone cry for you before, forest?
Forgive us, Mother, for raping you.

Ocean

By the Ocean,
enormous rocks
studded with shining pebbles.
The water seeps and sucks in
smooth harmony.
I can hear
the gulls
screaming in the
empty sky,
and a tug
churns its way
back to the harbor.
There is God
in the rocks,
the water,
the gulls and
the tug...
There is God
shining,
sweeping,
streaming...
God
chugging
thru' this world
un–noticed,
un–remarked.
God soaked Godself
in the world
when God fashioned it.

Hell's Streets

Out walking after midnight—
sad, lonely people
shuffling along the filthy streets,
strewn with garbage.
Eskimo Joe—with tears
in his eyes, caught unawares—
looking for a bush to sleep under.
Janice, with her bag of french-fries
hurrying down the station steps
to sleep fitfully.
Jim, wandering with his canvas bag
slung around him,
face contorted with tears
flowing freely.
The heavy black woman
shouting on the corner,
and I.
We stopped and talked awhile.

She was filled with anger,
resentment, pain—
we are white—
we are rich—
she, alienated, desperate.
She too, cannot fight the tears.
Ah, four adults
in the morning hours
weeping
among the garbage.

God's Wisdom

I have never seen so many wild flowers...
purple, white, yellow,
rising and falling,
swaying and dancing,
with God, whilst
the warm breeze hums,
and all, all of it,
is drenched in
rare sweet perfume.
Ah, God's breath!
"Show me your wisdom, God,"
I prayed.
"This," said God,
"is my wisdom."
And all around stretched
the great field of wild flowers
and glorious weeds
of all colors,
heights and variety.
The breeze gently rocked them,
bees, flies and colored butterflies
hovered, then burrowed
into the hearts
of the chosen flowers,
providing life and nurturing,
even to the little ones.
Tho' all so different,
together the mass of flowers
was splendid
in its variety.

But each alone was beautiful,
unique and standing proud,
sharing equally with all the others,
the loving breeze and
the warm sun.
In the wildness, in the freedom,
was splendid harmony,
and, from it all,
a glorious perfume rose,
as God breathed and danced
amongst the flowers.
"This," whispered the Perfume,
"is my wisdom."

The Grasshopper

I caught a grasshopper
between the slats of my louvered window.
I had watched her,
only a few minutes before
hopping, playing,
carefree as the sunlight
that caught the smooth lines
of her tapered body—
wood–like, brown and gold.
I smiled at her Spring freedom.
Then, distracted, I turned away—
just for a few moments.
And as I came back to the window
I idly turned the handle which
closed and snapped shut
my louvered window.
Too late,
the horror gripped me.
The grasshopper was caught
hanging helpless by its
long, delicate legs.
The large brown eyes
stunned in death's surprise.
I felt a great sadness,
a sense of enormous loss for
something so small, so fragile,
so free.
I was glad I had not heard
her silent scream.

Spring

The wet earth
is heavy with rain,
drenching
all its womb and
ladening it
with fertility.
Hidden in the darkness
little seeds
sprout and shift,
enlivened by
the dampness,
and begin to push
through the warm earth.
Fragile, brave,
and the only bright thing,
a new young leaf
stirs through the mud
birthing Spring.

A Place

I dream a place
for women
to come apart
to meet themselves
in a safe and nurturing space.
A place where women
who have never been alone,
or looked upon
their deep feminine selves
can be freed to sink
into the wombs of
their grandmothers,
their mothers,
themselves.
I dream a place
where all the cycles of
a woman's life
will be acknowledged
and celebrated
in tune with nature and
the rhythms of the earth.
I would like a place
where the weary,
the battered and the raped
will find healing
in herbs and touch and dance.
I dream a place
where women will sing and chant
beneath the full moon

and dance around
the dying embers,
a place
where the feminine will
be nurtured
and born again
into our world.

Ah, I dream a place
for virgin, mother and crone
to rise again
in fullness
with the moon.

Candle

Fruit

Flowers

The following prayers were written to be read aloud whilst gifts are brought ritualistically to the sacred table during a women's liturgical celebration.

In response to numerous requests for their publication from women who have attended celebrations led by the author, we print these prayers so that others may adapt or adopt them in creating their own worship services.

Candle

Mother God,
We bring to your table this gift of light:
A tiny flame which sputters into being
To dispel the darkness.
This flame represents the fire which burns
in our hearts,
it represents the heat of your love
for each one of us.

May this tiny flame set fire to the earth.
May we know the heat of your love,
May our hearts burn with love for one another
and for the planet on which we live.

Bless, O Mother of all life, our tiny flame.

Fruit

Mother God,
We bring to your table our gift of fruit.
Firm, ripe and round, of many colors
and varieties,
this basket of fruit glows in the fullness
of creation.

It is a sign of the richness of your blessing
on the earth,
this fruit, so sweet and so refreshing,
fills us and gives us energy and health.

May we too, Mother God, round and ripen
like this fruit.
May we, too, be filled with juice–iness.

Bless, O Mother of all life, our gift of fruit.

Flowers

Mother God,
We bring to your table our gift of flowers.
Colorful, of glorious shapes and design,
they dance together in splendid beauty.
Each one is unique in shape and
fragrance.
They bring joy to the eye—
they decorate the earth with color
and movement,
they are a sign of your gracious creativity
and a reflection of your beauty.

May these flowers, so pure and lovely,
remind us, Mother God,
of our own loveliness
and our own ability to shine and dance.

Bless, O Mother of all life,
our gift of flowers.

Water

Mother God,
We bring to your table our gift of water.
A tiny vessel filled with cool, clear water;
But with it, Mother God, we bring the entire
ocean.

This tiny vessel represents our thirst for
wholeness.
It represents the thirst of the world for love
and for meaning.

This water, Mother God, is a sign of hope
that we will be refreshed,
that the earth will bear fruit,
that our rain will be pure,
that our rivers and seas will be unpolluted
and that our hearts will be cleansed.

Bless, O Mother of all life, our vessel of
water.

Incense

Mother God,
We bring to your table our gift of incense.
From a distant eastern land, we bring this
sweet perfume which rises into the air and
fills our space with its sweetness.

As the air is perfumed with this incense,
may our lives be filled with fragrance,
may all we do rise before you,
filling the world with blessing.
May our fragrance, Mother God, sweeten
the earth.

Bless, O Mother of all life, our gift of incense.

Wine

Mother God,
we bring to your table our gift of wine.
Rich, red and full–bodied, it is the yield
of the berries which blossomed and burst
beneath the warmth of the sun.
It is a sign of joy and celebration.
It is a sign of community and sharing.

May we care for the tender bushes that
are meant to produce fruit.
May we ever be mindful of the need for
pruning,
for cutting back and for gathering in.
May we learn to rejoice in the fruit of our
labors.
And, may we share our overflowing cups
with one another.

Bless, O Mother of all life, our gift of wine.

Bread

Mother God,
we bring to your table our gift of bread.
This bread which comes from the rich moistness
and darkness of the earth,
which grew as wheat in the light of the sun
and became bread in the work of our hands.

This bread is a sign of hope for the world.
It represents our hope that we will share
the produce of the land and feed the hungry.
May this bread nurture and strengthen us in
our commitment to bring about a new world
of justice in which no one will ever go hungry.

Bless, O Mother of all life, our gift of bread.

The Offering

On my altar before God
there is a small plate with
three squares of cheese
and a slice of summer sausage,
half a glass of gin and tonic,
and a red candle burning.
They are like offerings, pathetic, human,
but very much me
and all I have at this time...

I think—how does God feel
about my cheese and sausage and gin?
Will God see them made holy,
because I think of Her
as I gaze on them
rather sadly, wistfully—
perhaps longing for incense,
starched cloth,
and the musky air
of a darkened church corner?

Will God receive my longing
and my dreams
through these lonely leftovers
which spiralled my little soul
to thoughts of love and redemption?

Cheese, summer sausage,
gin, and a red candle
burning, reflecting,
the fleeting glance
of an all-touching God.

Wholeness

Gather everything together
like the enveloping dusk.
Welcome it,
delight in it,
dreams and images,
memories,
hopes, pains—
Recall—
Relive—
Be–friend.
Let the past surge
forward into the gentle,
welcoming present,
and take each
far–wandered memory
into your bosom to kiss,
caress,
and claim your own,
your self.
Befriend,
reclaim your wholeness
and all the fragmented beauty
of who you are.

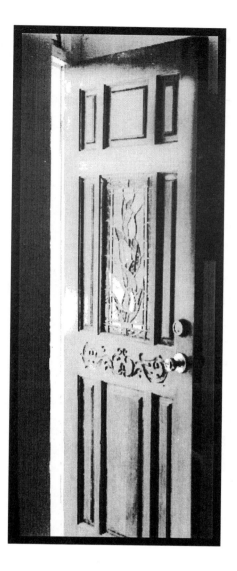

Called To Become

The Dance

His sturdy little body
leapt naked and nimble
to the music,
stomping in excitement,
turning, twisting,
posing in pure
self–delight,
his face radiant
with the joy
of free expression and
uninhibited tumbling play.
Absorbed,
soaking up the spontaneity
of being alive
he and the music
were one.
And I knew that
the dance was for God,
that the surging display
of joy and movement
was pure grace—
over–flowing
delighting in itself.
I felt a quiet nostalgia
for innocent leaping,
a mild envy of naked prayer.
I spiralled down the years
longing to remember
my dance,

but glimpsed only,
in the shadows, a dimmed Eden,
a fleeting shame
shrouded in gray disapproval
that would never
have dreamed nor dared
such naked music.
And God was bereft of
my dance.

Called To Say Yes

We are called to say yes
That the Kingdom might break through
To renew and to transform
Our dark and groping world.

We stutter and we stammer
To the lone God who calls
And pleads a New Jerusalem
In the bloodied Sinai Straits.

We are called to say yes
That honeysuckle may twine
And twist its smelling leaves
Over the graves of nuclear arms.

We are called to say yes
That children might play '
On the soil of Vietnam where the tanks
Belched blood and death.

We are called to say yes
That black may sing with white
And pledge peace and healing
For the hatred of the past.

We are called to say yes
So that nations might gather
And dance one great movement
For the joy of humankind.

We are called to say yes
So that rich and poor embrace
And become equal in their poverty
Through the silent tears that fall.

We are called to say yes
That the whisper of our God
Might be heard through our sirens
And the screams of our bombs.

We are called to say yes
To a God who still holds fast
To the vision of the Kingdom
For a trembling world of pain.

We are called to say yes
To this God who reaches out
And asks us to share
His crazy dream of love.

Letting Go

It is time to go.
I can smell it,
Breathe it
Touch it.
And something in me
Trembles.
I will not cry,
Only sit bewildered,
Brave and helpless
That it is time.
Time to go.
Time to step out
Of the world
I shaped and watched
Become.
Time to let go
Of the status and
The admiration.
Time to go.
To turn my back
On a life that throbs
With my vigor
And a spirit
That soared
Through my tears.
Time to go
From all I am
To all I have
Not yet become.

A Dream I Have Not Dreamt

There is a dream
I have not dreamt
A vision
I have not seen.

There is in me
A fearsome longing
Deep as primordial waters
And rooted in
The very womb
Of earth's fire.

There is in me
A life not become,
Stirring and reaching out
From the dreams and terrors
Of dark history.

There is in me
A fire not kindled,
Glowing like a lone
And passionate sentinel
Awaiting the dawn.

There is a dream
I have not dreamt
A vision
I have not seen.

Called To Become

You are called to become
A perfect creation.
No one is called to become
Who you are called to be.
It does not matter
How short or tall
Or thick—set or slow
You may be.
It does not matter
Whether you sparkle with life
Or are silent as a still pool,
Whether you sing your song aloud
Or weep alone in darkness.
It does not matter
Whether you feel loved and admired
Or unloved and alone
For you are called to become
A perfect creation.
No one's shadow
Should cloud your becoming,
No one's light
Should dispel your spark.
For the Lord delights in you,
Jealously looks upon you
And encourages with gentle joy
Every movement of the Spirit
Within you.

Unique and loved you stand,
Beautiful or stunted in your growth
But never without hope and life.
For you are called to become
A perfect creation.
This becoming may be
Gentle or harsh,
Subtle or violent,
But it never ceases,
Never pauses or hesitates,
Only *is*—
Creative force—
Calling you
Calling you to become
A perfect creation.

The Anointing

There were no crowds at my ordination
The church was cold and bare,
There was no bishop to bless and consecrate,
No organ music filled the air.
No solemn procession went before me,
No cross nor incense smell,
There were no songs nor incantation
And no pealing triumphant bell.

But I heard the children laughing
In the stench of the city slums.
And I heard the people sobbing
At the roaring of the guns.
And the stones cried out before me
As the sirens wailed and roared
And the blood of women and children
In the arid earth was poured.

There were no crowds at my ordination,
The church was cold and bare.
But the cries of the people gathered
And the songs of birds filled the air,
The wind blew cold before me,
The mountains rose and split,
The earth it shuddered and trembled
And a flame eternal was lit.

There were no crowds at my ordination,
The church was cold and bare,
But the Spirit breathed oh, so gently
In the free and open air,
She slipped through the walls and the barriers,
And from the stones and the earth She proclaimed:
Oh, see! My blind, blind people,
See Woman—whom I
Have ordained.

Disciple of Jesus

Disciple of Jesus, weary and silent,
aware, in the darkness of challenges failed
and longings unfilled,
remembering the passion that sent you forth,
young and bright and fired with hope.

Disciple of Jesus, weary and silent,
world unchanged, its darkness still deep,
dreams dispelled and visions blurred,
How is it now with you?

Trailing behind me the sparkle and fire
of early passion,
bruised and tender from love's long thrust.
Now is the finest, greatest moment
and now the ultimate death.

For I, Disciple of Jesus,
to stand before my God,
weary, silent, and all alone,
claiming only 'I was there.'

Passage

Like a splendid hawk
downed
my spirit wavers,
trembles,
then, stunned,
begins to fall—
plunging, plunging,
into depths
never encountered,
darkness not known.
The mighty wings are stilled,
the triumphant flight is over.
Now there is only
the soft yielding
earth
running wet with tears,
and land,
strange and uncharted,
waiting
unseeded
to spring
a new thing,
and circle
a deeper way.

I grieve for all I am called to be and am not.

There, where the forest fell
dark and deep
there was no path.
So I trod one.

Index of First Lines

Edwina Gateley

Born in Lancaster, England, Edwina has a teaching credential and a Masters Degree in Theological Studies. In the 1960s she worked in Uganda where she established a school for girls which became one of the most successful in the region. She went on to found the Volunteer Missionary Movement to prepare lay missionaries for work in the developing world. The VMM now has communities in Britain, Ireland, and the USA, and has sent over 1000 people to Africa, Papua New Guinea and South America.

In 1981 Edwina spent nine months of prayer and solitude in a hermitage in Illinois. This led her to the streets of Chicago, where for a year she walked with the homeless, the dispossessed, and women in prostitution. By 1984, she was able to found Genesis House, Chicago where women who are victims of prostitution and other abuse are welcomed and can feel safe, and where they can grow in self-respect and dignity. A second house for long–term care opened in Chicago in 1995.

Edwina's work has gained her recognition from many places: Catholic Woman of 1979 in England and Wales; The Spirit of St. Francis Award; The U.S. Catholic Mission Award; The Pope John XXIII Award, and so on. She is currently engaged in writing, advocating for women in prostitution, and giving talks, conferences and retreats in Britain, the U.S. and several other countries. Her publications include: *Psalms of A Laywoman* 1981, *I Hear A Seed Growing* 1990, *A Warm Moist Salty God* 1993, and a children's book: *God Goes on Vacation* 1995.

For information about speaking engagements, please write to

Maureen Donnelly
248 Carroll Ave. S.E.
Grand Rapids MI 49506